RIBBONS OF LOVE

RIBBONS OF LOVE

Heartfelt Poems of Faith and Grace

MARY ANN SULLIVAN

Purelilly Press

Contents

First Printing, 2024

ISBN: 979-8-9879012-7-4

Published by Purelilly Press Publishing
Huntsville, Texas

DEDICATED TO MY WONDERFUL CHILDREN

AND PRECIOUS GRANDCHILDREN

I

RIBBONS OF LOVE

Ribbons of love from my Savior,
Love of a special kind.
Healing, forgiveness, deliverance,
It is yours, and it is mine.
He shed it way back on Calvary,
Left it there for you and for me.
Ribbons still flowing today.
Just receive him and you will see.
There was no price he wouldn't pay,
And he already knew he couldn't stay.
He is the greatest gift ever given,
All wrapped up in precious red ribbons.

II

WONDERFUL GLORIOUS DIVINE

Jesus, you're wonderful, Jesus, you're mine.
Jesus, you're glorious, completely divine.
If I had a million years, or maybe even more,
I could not begin to tell of how you brought me over.
You've seen me through much toil and strife.
All the cares of my daily life.
The angels sing Hosanna all day long,
And one day I know I'll join in their song.
There will come a day I'll see your sweet face,
For I have been touched by your amazing grace.
All I can say is it is so fine,
And Jesus you're wonderful, glorious, and completely divine.

III

BEAUTIFUL MAN

I know whom I love, and I know who loves me.
That beautiful man from Galilee.
He is the rock of all ages and the King of all kings.
He will always be number one to me.
His name is Jesus, and I want you to know
That he will never, ever let you go.

IV

YOU ARE

You are the pearl in my oyster,
The bumble in my bee,
The sun in my daytime,
The leaves on every tree.
You are the stars that light the night.
They give me light to see.
Jesus, you are everything.
You are Lord to me.

8/10/2019

V

ADVISE

Yesterday is history.
Tomorrow is a mystery.
Today is a present, a gift from God.
So open it carefully.
Savor it slowly.
Taste and enjoy every moment
As if you were invited to a great banquet.
Do not rush through it, but let every moment touch you.
Allow yourself to be touched by the master.
His presence will change your life.

9/17/2019

VI

WORKING IN ME

Working in me, working in me.
Oh Lord, you are working in me.
All day long, and through the long night,
You are wonderfully working in me.
When I don't resist, and I give you the right,
You will always and forever fight my fight.
I am a champion, as all can see,
Because you have been gloriously working in me.
Now is the time, Lord, for all to see,
The wonderous things you have done in me.
So take my hand, Lord, as I take my stand,
To show your glory throughout the land.
Let's continue onward through the night,
And lead others to the light.
So, keep working in me,
Until I am completely and forever set free.

9/14/2018

VII

WONDERFUL MAN

I am in love with a wonderful man,
Who carries my scars around in his hands.
He received them one day back on Calvary,
when he was nailed to that cross for you and for me.
He didn't have to, but he took my place,
To keep me from dying in total disgrace.
His name is Jesus, and I love him so,
That I wanted to let you and the whole world know,
That if you will just call upon his precious name,
He will never let you be put to shame.
You see, Calvary was meant for you and for me,
Yet he accepted it, all so willingly.
I long for the day I see Jesus' face,
And lovingly give him a sweet embrace.
For no greater thing could anyone do,
Than lay down his life for me and for you.

5/27/2004

VIII

BEST FRIEND

Lord, you are divine, and you are strong.
I will love you, my whole life long.
In good times, even in bad,
You are the best friend I've ever had.
You are there when I am up, there when I am down,
There when no one else can even be found.
Lord, I feel you laugh when I am happy, cry when I am sad,
So again, I will say, "You are the best friend I've ever had."

IX

COME ALONG

Come along my children,
Come along with me.
Come along my children,
Just wait and see.
If you follow, I will lead you
Straightway to Calvary.
Satan had you bound as tight as you could be,
But I came down from Heaven, just to set you free!

X

HEAVEN IS NOT
FOR SALE

The enemy can't have Heaven,
Heaven is not for sale.
Although the enemy is running rampant,
He will not prevail.
His workers are drunk on power,
But they are bound for hell.
Again, I say to you, Satan,
"Heaven is not for sale!"

10/10/2023

Author's note:

While thinking about what was going on all around the world at that time, that is what I heard in my spirit.

XI

⁐

THE GREATEST STORY

Hundreds and hundreds of years ago
The greatest story that's ever been told,
Unfolded one day back on Calvary
When my Savior hung on that tree.
His name is Jesus of Nazareth,
And he died there for you and for me.
He could have summoned the angels
To free him that day,
But it was love that got in his way.
With the love of a father and a hatred for sin,
God told Satan, "You'll never win."
For when all's said and done,
With the blood of my son,
"I'll win humanity back again."

So just receive him today and the gift that he gave,
The cost was higher than we could pay.
But do not despair for Jesus is there,
And the price has already been paid.
Yes, do not despair for Jesus is there,
And YOUR price has already been paid.

Author's note:

When writing this, I heard it in my heart as a song inspired by the
Holy Spirit.

XII

A PRAYER

I pray, Lord, for your grace.
I pray Lord for your sweet embrace.
No one can love us like you do;
No other love so tried and found true.
I pray you kiss us with sweet morning dew,
And lead us along life's pathway with you.
This journey gets hard, Lord, so I humbly pray,
"Hold tightly to our hand, Lord, so we never stray."

XIII

MY BOY

My boy in the air in some unknown place,
May God keep you in His grace.
Jumping from airplanes in the sky,
It's good to know God sits on high.
I sit on the ground; I wonder and wait,
Until the day I know your fate.
Although you're a man now, it's hard for me
Not to open my door and see you swinging in a tree,
Running with a ball, or whatever your fancy might be.
You were sent to me from Heaven, like an angel from above,
And as you jump from airplanes,
May God hold you in His love!

Author's note:

My son enlisted in the Army, 82nd Airborne Division, Fort Bragg, North Carolina, from 1976 to 1980. He was 19 years old. Right now, 2023, my son is 66 years old, and I am 84, but, at the time, we were both young. He is my firstborn and my only son.

We were unsure of the future, and I was afraid for his life. Of course, as most mothers do, I prayed constantly. My prayer turned into a poem. At one point, I sent the poem to him. He told me he never made another jump without it.

By the way, he was a paratrooper and, up until that time, was the youngest "Jump Master" the Army ever had.

XIV

THE RING

You are an empty vessel; have tried everything,
But just accept Jesus, and I will give you a ring.
It is a ring of promise, I will plant it in your heart,
Reminding you always, that we will never part.
When I have gone to my Father, and you feel all alone,
This ring in your heart guarantees, in me you have a home.
A constant reminder of my love for you,
And it's telling you daily that my words are true.
So wear it with pride for the whole world to see,
That your heart and your life belong to me.

XV

LOVE

Love is gentle, love is kind.
Love is never far from my mind.
Jesus, Love's son, died in my place,
To save me from total disgrace.
His love spans the ages, been tried and found true.
He has opened his arms to me and to you.
Now there is no greater gift for our soon-coming king
Than to surrender our lives every day,
Assured, Jesus, will show us the way.
The way has been paved with a love so true.
It was laid out at Calvary, for me, and for you.

XVI

IF I WAS

If l was a Tree, in the wind I would sway.
If l was the Sand, on the beach I would lay.
If I was a Wolf, at the moon I would bay.
If I was a Scholar, eloquent words I would say.
But, since I am just human,
I thank God Almighty at the end of each day!

9/13/2007

XVII

ALL MY DAYS

If all my days were restored fresh and new,
There's nothing, Lord, that I'd rather do
Than live life to bring glory and honor to you.
The glory and honor you bestowed upon me,
When you gave your son so I could go free.
What an honor it is to carry your name,
And assurance in knowing I win in life's game.

9/13/2007

XVIII

AUNT FRANCES

A love so sweet and so divine.
I am yours and you are mine.
It reaches far, it reaches wide,
Across the span of time's great divide.
In between now and then,
I know someday we will meet again.
When it seems that all has been lost,
I direst remember Jesus bore the cross
So that you and I might live again,
Forever and ever at home with him.
So, I will not grieve, and I will not mourn.
There is a path that leads to that great door,
Through which we will live forevermore.

There will be no sorrow, no more tears,
Yes we will reign with him for a thousand years.
Although parting is great sorrow,
There is a promise of a great tomorrow.
I will just hold tightly to his hand,
And meet you in that far-off land.
With all my love, Mary Ann.

Author's note:

I wrote this at the passing of my precious aunt.

XIX

THE ONE WHO HOLDS TOMORROW

Thank you for the clouds, Lord,
Thank you for the rain.
I thank you for the sunshine,
I thank you for the pain.
I thank you for all the things I see and feel,
Because they let me know that you are truly real.
The road called life we travel is filled with winding ways,
But never let me forget that you have numbered all my days.
Some are filled with joy,
Some are filled with sorrow,
But never let me forget,
The one who holds tomorrow.

4/23/2007

XX

SHEKINA LIGHT

There will be no more darkness, no more night.
Let me be guided by your Shekina Light.
Radiant splendor, you're perfect and fair.
Let others know that I have been there.
Touched by your beauty, filled with your grace,
Let everyone see by the look on my face,
I have touched heaven for heavens touched me.
I want all to know how sweet it will be.
Lord, just let others see Jesus in me.
I fall to the ground, can't make a sound,
For Heaven's angels are all around.
The sound of their voices, the brush of their wings,
It just lets me know you're in everything.

XXI

YOUR WORD

I thank you for your word, Lord.
It is the bread of life and the living water too.
It is what sustains me and always gets me through.
It is the sweet connection between me and you.
Without your book of instruction
I wouldn't know where to go or what to do.
It is there to lead and guide me each step along the way.
It even has the words I need when it's time to pray.
Oh, how I love your word, Lord, it has given life to me.
Without it I dare not even think of where or what I'd be.
So, again, I thank you, Lord, for helping me this day,
For in your word there is instruction on what to do and say.
In the midnight hour, or in the light of day,
I thank you, Lord, that you are here to lighten up my way.
I know you'll never leave me when I hold tightly to your hand,
As together we spread your word throughout all the land.

XXII

MY JESUS

I love my Jesus, oh yes, I do.
I love my Jesus 'cause he's tried and true.
He was tried and found guilty; he took the blame.
He died on that cross for my guilt and shame.
I can never repay him with works on my part,
But I intend to love him with all my heart.
Thank you, sweet Jesus, for that gift of love.
It lives inside me like a sweet mourning dove.
I will strive daily to live without strife,
Preparing one day to be part of your wife.
Yes, the bride of Christ is what I long to be.
A part of your body for eternity!

4/21/2004

XXIII

HOLY SPIRIT

Stir in me Holy Spirit,
Blow across my heart.
Breathe your breath of life in me
For I'm needing a fresh start.
Life without you, Holy Spirit,
Is so empty and so bare.
My heart longs to know
That you are really there.
I've tried the things of this world
And came out feeling all alone,
So come, Holy Spirit.
Make my heart your home.
I can't live without you.
I won't even try.
Without you, Holy Spirit,
I would surely die!

10/15/2000

XXIV

⚮

TRIED AND TRUE

I have a friend and in him,
There is no end to what he and I can do.
He is as sweet as a dove,
Filled with nothing but love.
He is my savior, and I can say,
He has been tried and found so completely true.

9/13/2005

XXV

LORD AND SAVIOR

My Lord and Savior,
My soon-coming king.
My Lord and Savior,
You are my everything.
I will forever trust you,
And give you my life,
Through all life's troubles,
Trials, and strife.
Come Lord be with me.
Come Lord, and stay.
Forever be with me.
Yes, Lord, I pray.

XXVI

KNOW WHO I LOVE

I know who I love, and I know who loves me.
He's that beautiful man from Galilee.
He is the rock of all ages, the King of all kings.
One thing I know, he'll never leave me.
He rescued my heart one stormy night,
And promised He would always hold me tight.
So, I will hold tightly to his dear hand,
And promise that I will take a stand.
I will live for him and do what is right.
I will stick to the end and fight the good fight.

XXVII

THE RIGHT CHOICE

Have you made the right choice?
You must walk in the light,
Or you will fall in the night.
The time is coming, my friend,
We are nearing the end.
So please do not fight.
Just do what is right.
God has had a plan from beginning to end.
His way is straight; it does not bend.
Choose Jesus today. He'll not let you stray!
Remember, he said, "I AM the way!"

9/16/2013

XXVIII

A PEARL

A pearl is a thing of beauty, grown from a grain of sand.
The oyster is its mother who holds it in her hand.
Through all the roughness of life's ocean
She polishes it with love
Till it's a thing of beauty as great as a mother's love.
You are the pearl from my ocean, a jewel of the rarest kind.
Each time you wear your pearls,
Please keep me in your heart and in your mind.

Author's note:

Written for my daughter, Marilyn, on August 17, 1993. She was receiving her doctorate degree in political science at the tender age of 28; a rare occurrence, and my pearls were the rarest thing I had to gift her with.

XXIX

PRECIOUS

Precious Heavenly Father,
Precious Jesus, too,
Precious Holy Spirit,
Your love is always true.
There is no one like you,
Above or down below,
So let me declare it loud and clear
That I also love you so!

XXX

ONE AND ONLY

You are my one and only.
You are my night and day.
God, my Abba Father,
I will follow you come what may.
Speak to my heart, my Father.
My promise is to obey.
Show me, Heavenly Father,
The error of my ways.
I endeavor to seek you
In all I say and do,
So, Father God, please help me
To always follow through.

Evening of 9/16/2023

XXXI

SWEET JESUS, LORD AND SAVIOR

My Lord and Savior, my soon coming King.
My sweet Jesus, you are my everything.
I wish I had the words to tell,
How you saved me from an eternal hell.
My head is full, and I could cry,
Because you love me, and I don't know why.
All the things that I've done wrong,
Still, you love me, oh so strong.
I want you to know through stumbling and fear,
You are my rock, and I hold you so dear.
At times, I can't find the words to pray,
But walking with you, Lord, makes my day.

3/15/2017

XXXII

⊛

CUT YOUR DISTRACTIONS AND FOCUS

Cut your distractions; give your troubles to the Lord.
Practice every day, and it won't really seem that hard.
We have an enemy that is roaring loud and strong,
But his days are numbered, and it won't be very long.
Our Lord and Savior Jesus will be coming with a shout,
So, focus on that day, casting all distractions out.

Author's note:

I wrote this poem for the singles ministry conference at Praise Chapel;
July 17, 2021.

XXXIII

THE STRUGGLE IS REAL

The struggle is real! It can be tough and long,
But I am with you and will keep you strong.
The attacks may be coming from the left and the right,
But remember I am with you through the long dark night.
All your struggles will come to an end.
In my will, you'll find your dearest friend.
I have never left you. I never will.
Your victory is coming just over the hill.
As surely as day follows night,
Your future in Me is very bright.

Author's note:

I wrote this poem for the Mother's Day celebration; March 11, 2023.

XXXIV

❦

RAPTURE

I am going in the rapture, and it won't be the end.
I will return someday, with my Lord and friend,
To rule and reign forever, for he gave me a promise
That I would meet him in the sky.
Death has been defeated! So, I will never die.
No one knows the day or hour, but it is very near.
The God of all creation has made it all so clear.
So, keep your eyes on Heaven,
And your heart fixed on him.
The road's been rough and rocky,
Filled with many twists and turns,
But in the heart of God, your salvation churns.
He'll not leave nor forsake you; he sees into your heart.
You see, at the great creation, he knew you'd have a part.
So, spend your time in wisdom,
While waiting for his kingdom.
Be mindful that the Lord will never let you down,
And in the storehouse of Heaven, for you, he has a crown.

XXXV

MOTHERS WEARING HATS

I am a mother wearing many hats,
At times wondering, who I am and where I'm at!
I have traveled to and fro.
Dear God, which way do I go?!
Without you Lord I would be lost,
But you stepped in and paid the cost.
I will wear my hat, whatever it may be,
For in you, Lord, there is sweet victory.

Author's note:

I wrote this poem for a Mother's Day celebration at Praise Chapel Church.

XXXVI

LIFE'S ROADS

Life's roads are rocky,
You can be sure that it's true,
But Jesus paved them all
With love for me and for you!

XXXVII

DAUGHTERS MOTHERS GRANDMOTHERS

Daughters, Mothers, and Grandmothers all in a row.
All seeking to find their purpose; which way will they go?
Representing all stages of life,
Each having its own strife.
For the older, it's nearing its end,
The younger, it's about to begin.
But the one in the middle touches them all.
Let's all join hands so that none of us fall.
Teaching and learning keep us all strong,
And we need each other all day long.
We are all God's children, different stages of life.
Keep it all centered on him, and he will handle life's strife.

Author's note:

I wrote this poem for the Mother Daughter Tea event at Praise Chapel;
September 1, 2023.

XXXVIII

SOUL CRY

Oh Lord, my soul cries out to you.
I'm in a desperate situation.
My heart is heavy, and only you, oh God,
Can bring your people out of bondage.
We are trapped by our mouths.
We fall into temptation.
In the day of evil, the snare of the fowler
Beseeched us to come, and we came.
Help us, oh Lord!
Your people are looking to see
If you are there,
And if you still care.
I seek your face and a gentle touch.
Just a word from you, Lord,
That you care so very much.

6/21/2001

XXXIX

GIVE YOUR LIFE

Give your life to Jesus;
Give him your life today.
Give your life to Jesus,
And He'll teach you how to pray.
In his word, there is wisdom;
In his word, there is life.
In his word, there is liberty,
Free from all fear and strife.
So, give your heart to Jesus;
Oh! Give him your heart, I pray.
When you give him your heart,
He'll never depart,
And you'll have a friend who will stay.

XL

HIS SPLENDOR

I behold your splendor, Lord Jesus;
My heart sees your face.
There is such majesty,
Power, and grace.
Heaven's angels could never tell,
Of all you have waiting,
When we meet you there!

XLI

THANK YOU

I thank you for your word, Lord.
It is the bread of life, and the living water, too.
It is what sustains me and always gets me through.
It is the sweet connection between me and you.
Without your book of instructions
I wouldn't know where to go, or, what to do.
It is there to lead and guide me each step along the way.
It even has the words I need when it's time to pray.
Oh, how I need your word, Lord! It has given life to me.
Without it, I dare not even think, of where or what I'd be.
So again, I thank you, Father, for helping me on this day.
For in your word there are instructions on what to do and say.
In the midnight hour, or in the light of day,
I thank you, Heavenly Father, that you're here to light my way.
I know you'll never leave me as I hold tightly to your hand.
As together we spread your word throughout all the land.

XLII

NOTHING CHANGES

Nothing in this world changes.
There's always right and wrong.
Jesus is the "Light" I live by.
He's with me all day long.
Jesus is the light I live by.
He always keeps me strong.
He gives me strength in times of weakness.
He never ever fails in my darkest hour.
His precious love prevails.
Although nothing in this world changes,
And there's always right and wrong.
Jesus is the lighthouse,
And he keeps shining on and on.